For Anna and Nathan

First published in the United States of America by Jessica Nagelkirk

Copyright © 2022 by Jessica Nagelkirk

All rights reserved. No part of this book may be reproduced or used in any manner without written permission of the copyright owner except for the use of quotations in a book review.

First paperback edition March 2022

Illustrations and cover art by Olga Seregina
Layout by Jessica Nagelkirk

ISBN 978-1-7923-8491-2

facebook.com/JessicaNagelkirkChildrensBookAuthor

Blueberry Pancakes

Written by Jessica Nagelkirk
Illustrated by Olga Seregina

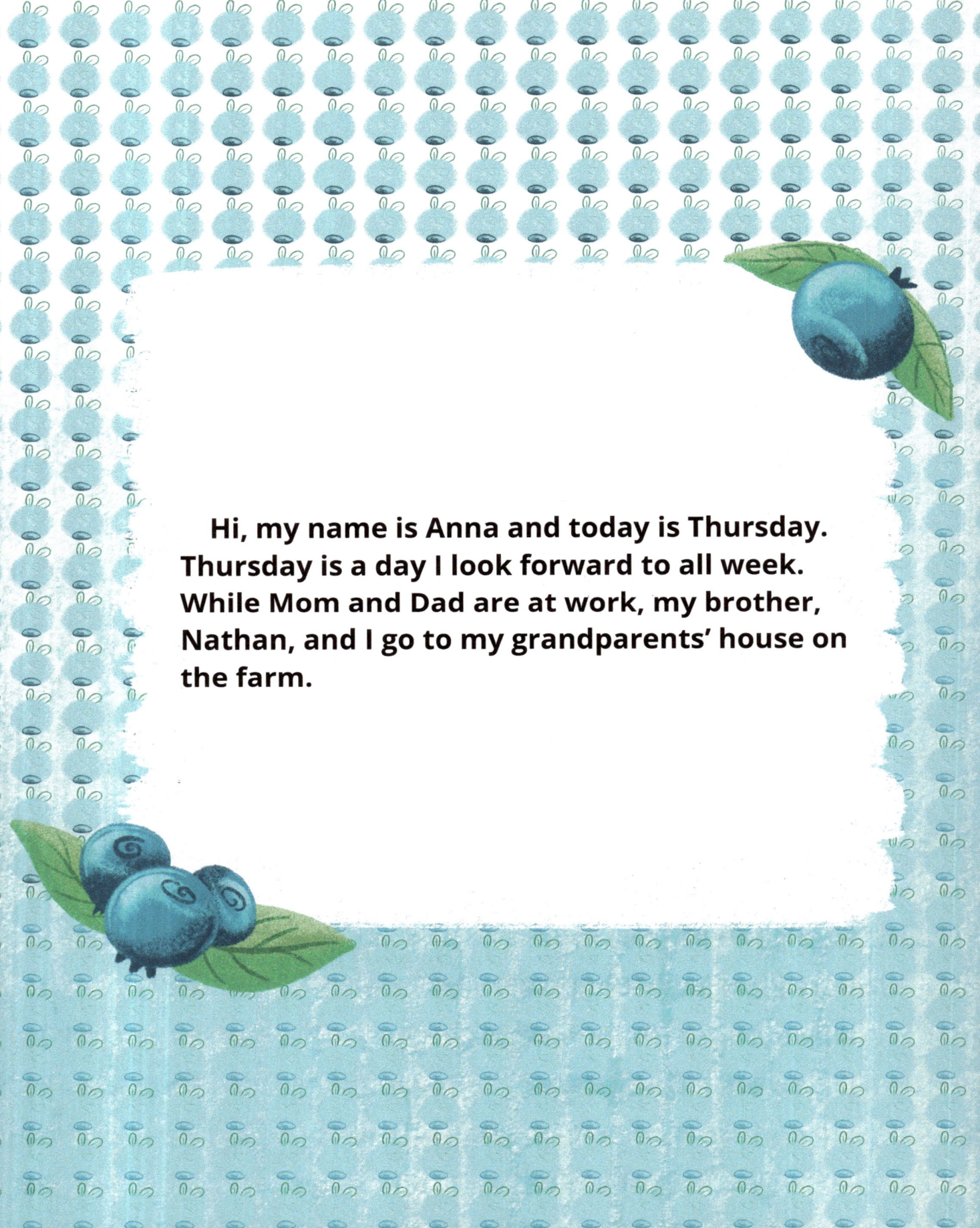

Hi, my name is Anna and today is Thursday. Thursday is a day I look forward to all week. While Mom and Dad are at work, my brother, Nathan, and I go to my grandparents' house on the farm.

We have fun at their house doing different activities. Grandma keeps us entertained by coloring and doing puzzles with us. We like to play with dolls and daddy's old tractors too.

Sometimes she even lets us take the cushions off her couch to jump on them. Occasionally, we forget to take the cushions off the couch before we start to bounce.

Grandpa usually tries to stay outside and work on the farm while we are over. He says we are too much fun for him to handle.

After all the playing, our tummies start to grumble. We ask Grandma to make one of her yummy treats. Homemade blueberry pancakes are one of our favorites. Lucky for us, my dad grows blueberries in the field next to Grandma and Grandpa's house.

In the summer, we walk the rows of blueberry bushes with buckets to pick fresh berries for our pancakes. We frequently see wild rabbits, deer, or turkeys nibbling berries off the bushes for a tasty snack. They always run away before we can get too close. Grandma says they get spooked by our laughing and running.

The blueberry patch is a special place. It feels like entering a candyland jungle of lush green bushes decorated with colorful clusters of green, pink, purple, and blue candies. The best part about this juicy candy is we can eat as much as we want. Grandma says the blueberries are actually good at keeping our bodies healthy and strong.

In the mornings, when the dew is still on the leaves, the bushes sparkle in the sun. The only sounds are birds chirping, leaves on nearby trees dancing in the wind, and berries plip-plopping into our buckets.

Grandma reminds us to only pick the bluest blueberries because they are the sweetest. The green, pink, and purple ones are still growing and ripening. I tried a purple berry (because it's my favorite color), but it tasted sour and scrunched my face up all funny.

Nathan and I don't drop too many berries into our buckets. We are busy popping them into our mouths as fast as we are picking them. Grandma just smiles at us while she continues to pluck handfuls of berries and place them into her bucket. She tells us stories from when she picked these same bushes as a little girl. Her bucket gets full really fast.

Back in Grandma's kitchen, we are excited to mix our ingredients together for our pancakes. Grandma helps us measure sugar, eggs, milk, and flour in a big bowl.

Nathan and I take turns stirring the batter. Sometimes we spill some over the sides of the bowl. Grandma gently tells us to slow down and cleans up the spill with a rag.

We add the sweet blueberries last and carefully stir them into the batter trying hard not to squash them. Grandma pours puddles of slightly purple tinted batter onto the hot griddle. We watch for bubbles to pop up into the batter. I search for the biggest bubble. Grandma flips them over to cook the other side; then they are ready to eat.

Of course, no pancake is complete without maple syrup. We let Grandma help us pour some on our pancakes so we don't use too much.

Grandpa comes back inside after feeding the cows to eat some blueberry pancakes too. As we cut into the pancakes, the blueberries ooze like lava seeping from a volcano.

I can't wait until next Thursday when we come to Grandma's house again. Maybe next time we can pick blueberries for muffins.

Grandma's Blueberry Pancake Recipe:

Ingredients:
1 ¼ C sifted flour
2 tsps. baking powder
2 tbsp. sugar
3/4 teaspoon salt
1 egg, well beaten
1 C milk
3 tbsp. melted shortening
1 C fresh blueberries

Directions:
Sift flour, baking powder, sugar, and salt. Combine egg, milk, and melted shortening. Slowly add flour mixture. Stir only until dry ingredients are moist but still lumpy. Add blueberries and fold in gently. Bake on hot griddle. Turn only once – wait until top side is covered with bubbles.

About the Author

Jessica Nagelkirk lives in Holland, Michigan with her husband and two kids. She currently works part time as a general sonographer. After reading hundreds of picture books to her own children, she decided to write one of her own. *Blueberry Pancakes* is Jessica's first children's book.

www.ingramcontent.com/pod-product-compliance
Lightning Source LLC
LaVergne TN
LVHW072018060526
838200LV00060B/4698